W9-ADU-531

Praise for *Abraham Lincoln: Quotes, Quips, and Speeches*

"An easy and enjoyable introduction to one of America's greatest presidents and heroes."
—*Tom Schwartz, historian emeritus for the state of Illinois*

"Gordon Leidner provides readers with a toothsome smorgasbord of Abraham Lincoln's wit and wisdom. This volume is an excellent introduction to the Great Emancipator's humanity, philosophy, humor, and eloquence. To supplement Lincoln's own memorable words, Leidner adds judicious comments by such eminent figures as Frederick Douglass, Theodore Roosevelt, and Booker T. Washington."
—*Michael Burlingame, Chancellor Naomi B. Lynn Distinguished Chair in Lincoln Studies, University of Illinois Springfield*

"Abraham Lincoln had the God-given talent to express himself in words that the people felt and understood. [This] book enables readers to sample and touch the greatness of Lincoln through his letters, public papers, and speeches."
—*Edwin C. Bearss, historian emeritus, National Park Service*

THE
FOUNDING
FATHERS
Quotes, Quips, AND *Speeches*

GORDON LEIDNER

Editor

CUMBERLAND HOUSE

Copyright © 2013 by Gordon Leidner
Cover and internal design © 2013 by Sourcebooks, Inc.
Cover image © *Declaration of Independence* by John Trumbull, 1817, public domain

Sourcebooks and the colophon are registered trademarks of Sourcebooks, Inc.

All rights reserved. No part of this book may be reproduced in any form or by
any electronic or mechanical means including information storage and retrieval
systems—except in the case of brief quotations embodied in critical articles or
reviews—without permission in writing from its publisher, Sourcebooks, Inc.

All photos courtesy of the Library of Congress.

This publication is designed to provide accurate and authoritative information
in regard to the subject matter covered. It is sold with the understanding that
the publisher is not engaged in rendering legal, accounting, or other professional
service. If legal advice or other expert assistance is required, the services of a com-
petent professional person should be sought. —*From a Declaration of Principles
Jointly Adopted by a Committee of the American Bar Association and a Committee of
Publishers and Associations*

Published by Cumberland House, an imprint of Sourcebooks, Inc.
P.O. Box 4410, Naperville, Illinois 60567-4410
(630) 961-3900
Fax: (630) 961-2168
www.sourcebooks.com

Library of Congress Cataloguing-in-Publication data is on file with the publisher.

Printed and bound in China.
LEO 10 9 8

To our grandchildren

Contents

Preface

THE FOUNDING FATHERS of the United States of America led a revolution that was truly unique in world history. Prior to the establishment of the United States, the majority of the nations of the world had been ruled by monarchies or oligarchies. Democratic governments had been few, and virtually all of them had failed. The voices of the common people were rarely heard or heeded.

The Founding Fathers: Quotes, Quips, and Speeches narrates the Revolution story through the words of men who respected the abilities of the common people. The majority of the quotes are from men who are generally recognized as the primary Founding Fathers of the United States: George Washington, Thomas Jefferson, John Adams, Patrick Henry, James Madison, Alexander Hamilton, Benjamin Franklin, and Thomas Paine. There are also several quotes from other men who are frequently recognized as founders, such as Samuel Adams, John Jay, Gouverneur Morris, and George Mason.

Also included are a few quotes from American soldiers who, in risking their lives, made their invaluable contribution to the success of the Rebellion. To help explain the context of the Revolution, there are a handful of quotes from British generals and political leaders.

The Founders created three world-changing documents: the Declaration of Independence, the Constitution, and the Bill of Rights. Excerpts of the Declaration of Independence and the entire Bill of Rights are included, along with selected speeches, at the end of the book.

Each chapter begins with a short introduction to provide some background for the quotes that follow. To improve the quotes' readability, minor changes were sometimes made to correct capitalization and punctuation errors, but spelling errors were usually left unchanged. The Internet offers many popular quotes attributed to the Founding Fathers that are, in fact, spurious. A sincere effort was made to make certain that erroneous quotes are not included, as evidenced by the endnotes in the back of the book.

I hope the reader derives as much pleasure in reading the original words of the Founders as I had in assembling them. You are invited to enter into the "Spirit of '76" and hear the voices of people who changed the world.

—*Gordon Leidner*

Background

THE SEEDS OF the American Revolution began germinating in the early 1760s, after Britain defeated France in what is known in America as the French and Indian War. Under the pretext that the colonies should pay a larger proportion of the costs of their defense, Parliament sought to increase British authority by imposing a series of new laws, duties, and taxes. Beginning with the Stamp Act of 1765 and continuing with the Quartering Act, the Townsend Acts, and finally a series of laws that became known as the Intolerable Acts, the decade after the end of the French and Indian War became one of increasing animosity between Great Britain and her subjects in the American colonies.

Since America lacked official representation in the British Parliament, many colonists considered these laws to be an egregious violation of their rights as Englishmen. Colonists became increasingly hostile to the actions of British-appointed governors and judiciary, believing they were too willing to sacrifice justice on behalf of the King. The influence of the Church of England was also seen as unfair, and American Baptist, Congregationalist, and Presbyterian ministers became more outspoken in their criticism of government-sanctioned religion.

Impatient with Parliament's imposition of authority, American colonists elected the First Continental Congress in 1774 and appealed to King George III for his intervention. These appeals were ignored. Conflict broke out between American militia and British troops on April 19, 1775, in skirmishes at Lexington and Concord, Massachusetts. Two months later, the Continental Congress commissioned George Washington commander in chief of the Continental Army, and the Battle of Bunker Hill in Boston became the first major military engagement between British and American forces. Finally, in October 1775, George III declared the colonies "in rebellion" and the members of Congress traitors.

On July 4, 1776, the representatives from

the thirteen colonies of the Second Continental Congress approved the Declaration of Independence, permanently severing ties with Great Britain and proclaiming the United States of America as a sovereign nation.

However, inherent weaknesses of the Continental Congress became obvious as the Revolutionary War progressed. The Congress had no authority to obtain revenue through taxes, regulate trade, or enforce treaties. These limitations resulted in a highly inflationary economy and an inability to pay the nation's bills, including the wages for American soldiers.

The nascent American army, under the gifted leadership skills of George Washington, fought surprisingly well. In spite of being frequently outnumbered, poorly supplied, and up against one of the world's strongest military powers, they successfully fought a war of attrition that lasted nearly eight years. Washington's talents were challenged by the perpetual need for recruitment and supply of troops, the necessity of avoiding battles of annihilation by superior British armies, and the petty politics of Congress. Although suffering numerous military defeats, Washington, the armies under his command, and America's French allies gained a number of strategic victories. These included the battles of Trenton and Princeton, New Jersey, in 1776; Saratoga, New York, in 1777; and Yorktown, Virginia, in 1781. The latter two battles resulted in the surrender of two entire British armies. After British General Cornwallis's surrender at Yorktown in October 1781, it became obvious to Britain that they could not defeat America militarily. Britain accepted the terms of the Treaty of Paris on September 3, 1783, officially ending the Revolutionary War and recognizing the United States as an independent nation.

At war's end, the Continental Congress was the sole organ of the national government. In addition to the shortcomings previously mentioned, it had neither a national court to interpret laws nor an executive branch to enforce them. These weaknesses made it obvious to American political leaders that the establishment of a stronger central government with expanded powers was critical to the survival of the nation.

Twelve of thirteen state legislatures sent delegates to the Constitutional Convention in Philadelphia in May 1787. George Washington presided over this convention, and many of the nation's most gifted leaders, including James Madison, Alexander Hamilton, and Benjamin Franklin, hammered out the Constitution over the ensuing weeks. Questions over a strong central government versus states' rights and how the power in federal government should be shared were vigorously debated. The result was a centralized form of government that divided power between three branches: legislative, judicial, and executive. The federal government gained the essential powers that the Continental Congress had lacked, and the states retained a large degree of autonomy.

Thirty-nine delegates of the Convention signed the Constitution on September 17, 1787, and sent it to the states for ratification. During the ensuing months, the Constitution was hotly debated by Federalists, who supported it, and Antifederalists, who did not. Federalist leaders James Madison, Alexander Hamilton, and John Jay anonymously wrote a series of eighty-five articles, which are known today as *The Federalist Papers*, promoting its ratification. The Federalist arguments prevailed when eleven states ratified the Constitution, and it went into effect March 4, 1789. Concerned with limiting the power of the government and securing the liberty of citizens, many of the states had ratified the Constitution contingent on the adoption of a bill of rights. Pursuant to this, James Madison proposed twelve amendments. Ten of these were ratified by the states, and their adoption was certified December 15, 1791. These first ten amendments are known today as the Bill of Rights.

The Constitution is the oldest written charter of organic law of any major government in the world. In over two hundred years of its existence, only seventeen additional amendments have been passed subsequent to the Bill of Rights.

Noteworthy is the fact that, originally, the Bill of Rights implicitly excluded the rights of Native Americans, African Americans, and women. These omissions would later result in war and significant civil strife in America.

The Revolution

THE AMERICAN REVOLUTION took place in the hearts and minds of the people long before the first shots were fired. Their leaders had inspired them with visions of independence from monarchical rule—a type of government they frequently called "tyranny." Americans became skeptical of the British government's integrity and suspected that neither the King, Parliament, nor the Royal Governors had their best interests at heart. Nevertheless, allegiance to the Crown died hard. Despite unpopular taxes, forced quartering of troops, and actions of a judiciary system that gave preferential treatment to loyalist officials, the Continental Congress made more than one effort to appeal to the King. When George III decided to send more troops to enforce the law, the kindling for the fire was placed. It needed only a spark to start a war.

But what do we mean by the American Revolution? Do we mean the American war? The Revolution was effected before the war commenced. The Revolution was in the minds and hearts of the people; a change in their religious sentiments, of their duties and obligations…This radical change in the principles, opinions, sentiments, and affections of the people was the real American Revolution.[1]

—*John Adams*

Our petitions have been slighted; our remonstrances have produced additional violence and insult; our supplications have been disregarded; and we have been spurned, with contempt, from the foot of the throne![2]

—*Patrick Henry*

Believe me, dear Sir: there is not in the British empire a man who more cordially loves a union with Great Britain than I do. But, by the God that made me, I will cease to exist before I yield to a connection on such terms as the British Parliament propose; and in this, I think I speak the sentiments of America.[3]

—*Thomas Jefferson*

It has been said that…the King, his ministry, and Parliament, will not endure to hear the Americans talk of their rights. But Americans will not endure in silence the slow erosion of those freedoms which make them proud of the name of Englishmen.[4]

—*John Adams*

We have…given Britain one more chance, one opportunity more, of recovering the friendship of the colonies; which, however, I think she has not sense enough to embrace, and so I conclude she has lost them forever.[5]

—*Benjamin Franklin*

We have boasted the protection of Great Britain, without considering that her motive was interest not attachment; that she did not protect us from our enemies on our account, but from her enemies on her own account.[6]

—*Thomas Paine*

The [British] covenanted with the first settlers of this country, that we should enjoy all the Libertys of free natural born subjects of Great Britain. They were not contented to have all the benefits of our trade, in short to have all our earnings, but they wanted to make us hewers of wood and drawers of water. Their Parliament have declared that they will have a right to tax us & Legislate for us, in all cases whatever—now certainly if they have a right to take one shilling from us without our consent, they have a right to all we possess; for it is the birthright of an Englishman, not to be taxed without consent of himself, or representatives.[7]

—*Paul Revere*

Caesar had his Brutus; Charles the First his Cromwell; and [King] George the Third may profit by their example.[8]

—*Patrick Henry*

It is inconsistent with the spirit of the common law and of the essential fundamental principles of the British constitution that we should be subject to any tax imposed by the British Parliament; because we are not represented in that assembly.[9]

—*John Adams*

Resistance to tyranny becomes the Christian and social duty of each individual…Continue steadfast and, with a proper sense of your dependence on God, nobly defend those rights which heaven gave, and no man ought to take from us.[10]

—*John Hancock*

Patrick Henry
(May 29, 1736–June 6, 1799)

*P*atrick Henry was an attorney, politician, soldier, planter, and one of the most inspiring orators of the revolutionary era. He was a leader in the opposition to the Stamp Act of 1765, and shortly before the war began, his famous "give me liberty or give me death!" speech was inspirational in the Virginia House of Burgesses' decision to contribute troops to the war effort. Henry served two terms as postcolonial governor of Virginia, which was his highest political office. A strong Antifederalist and proponent of states' rights, Henry opposed the adoption of the U.S. Constitution because he thought it gave too much power to the federal government. Concerned for the rights of individuals, he helped in the adoption of the Bill of Rights. Thomas Jefferson summed up Henry's talents when he said of him: "He spoke as Homer wrote."[11]

For God's sake, let us come to a final separation...The birthday of a new world is at hand.[12]
                    —*Thomas Paine*

The Eyes of all our Countrymen are now upon us, and we shall have their blessings, and praises, if happily we are the instruments of saving them from the Tyranny mediated against them. Let us therefore animate and encourage each other, and shew the whole world, that a Freeman contending for liberty on his own ground is superior to any slavish mercenary on earth.[13]

—*George Washington*

☆☆☆

Objects of the most stupendous magnitude, and measure in which the lives and liberties of millions yet unborn are intimately interested, are now before us. We are in the very midst of a revolution the most complete, unexpected and remarkable of any in the history of nations.[14]

—*John Adams*

Rebellion to tyrants is obedience to God.[15]
—*Thomas Jefferson*

All men have a right to remain in a state of nature as long as they please; and in case of intolerable oppression, civil or religious, to leave the society they belong to, and enter into another.[16]
—*Samuel Adams*

Everything that is right or reasonable pleads for separation. The blood of the slain, the weeping voice of nature cries, 'tis time to part![17]
—*Thomas Paine*

Shall we gather strength by irresolution and inaction? Shall we acquire the means of effectual resistance by lying supinely on our backs, and hugging the delusive phantom of hope, until our enemies shall have bound us hand and foot? Sir, we are not weak, if we make a proper use of those means which the God of nature has placed in our power."[18]

—*Patrick Henry*

If there must be trouble, let it be in my day, that my child may have peace.[19]

—*Thomas Paine*

The God who gave us life, gave us liberty at the same time; the hand of force may destroy, but cannot disjoin them.[20]

—*Thomas Jefferson*

Liberty must at all hazards be supported. We have a right to it, derived from our Maker. But if we had not, our fathers have earned and bought it for us, at the expense of their ease, their estates, their pleasure, and their blood.[21]

—*John Adams*

It is in vain, sir, to extenuate the matter. Gentlemen may cry, peace, peace—but there is no peace. The war is actually begun! The next gale that sweeps from the north will bring to our ears the clash of resounding arms! Our brethren are already in the field! Why stand we here idle? What is it that gentlemen wish? What would they have? Is life so dear or peace so sweet as to be purchased at the price of chains and slavery? Forbid it, Almighty God. I know not what course others may take, but as for me, give me liberty or give me death![22]

—*Patrick Henry*

The sacred rights of mankind are not to be
rummaged for, among old parchments, or
musty records. They are written, as with a sun
beam, in the whole volume of human nature,
by the hand of the divinity itself; and can never
be erased or obscured by mortal power.[23]

—Alexander Hamilton

But where; say some, is the King of America?
I'll tell you, friend, He reigns above.[24]

—Thomas Paine

The right to freedom being the gift of God
Almighty, it is not in the power of man to alien-
ate this gift and voluntarily become a slave.[25]

—Samuel Adams

Can the liberties of a nation be thought secure when we have removed their only firm basis, a conviction in the minds of the people that these liberties are the gift of God? That they are not to be violated but with His wrath? Indeed, I tremble for my country when I reflect that God is just; that His justice cannot sleep forever.[26]

—*Thomas Jefferson*

But a Constitution of Government once changed from Freedom, can never be restored. Liberty, once lost, is lost forever.[27]

—*John Adams*

We have it in our power to begin the world over again.[28]

—*Thomas Paine*

Suppose the colonies do abound in men, what does that signify? They are raw, undisciplined, cowardly men.[29]

> —*Lord Sandwich, Britain's First Lord of the Admiralty*

The dye is now cast; the colonies must either submit or triumph. I do not wish to come to severer measures, but we must not retreat.[30]

> —*King George III*

The war is inevitable—and let it come! I repeat it, sir, let it come![31]

> —*Patrick Henry*

2

The Rebellion

THE FIRST SHOTS of the American Revolutionary War rang out on April 19, 1775. Seven hundred British soldiers had marched out from Boston, Massachusetts, in search of a cache of weapons. In Lexington, they encountered seventy-five militia troops who had assembled in response to a summons by Paul Revere. The American soldiers, commanded by Captain John Parker, skirmished briefly with the superior British force, and then the Redcoats continued their march to Concord. There they met a force of about five hundred American militia and minutemen. After a short battle, the British withdrew, suffering heavy casualties in their long retreat to Boston. Two months later, George Washington was placed in command of the Continental Army. He led his troops through eight years of bitter conflict before Britain sued for peace.

Stand your ground; don't fire unless fired upon, but if they mean to have a war, let it begin here.[32]

>   —*American Captain John Parker [at Lexington]*

Fire, for God's sake, fellow soldiers, fire![33]

>   —*Major John Buttrick [ordering the first American fire at Concord]*

I have not yet begun to fight![34]

>   —*John Paul Jones [USS* Bonhomme Richard *captain]*

I have been called upon by the unanimous voice of the Colonies to take command of the Continental Army—an honor I neither sought after, nor desired, as I am thoroughly convinced that it requires greater abilities, and more experience, than I am master of…but the partiality of the Congress, joined to a political motive, really left me without a choice.[35]

—*George Washington*

My God! These fellows have done more work in one night than I could make my army do in three months![36]

—*British General William Howe [after seeing breastworks thrown up by American troops overnight in Boston]*

Men, you know you are all marksmen, you know you can take a squirrel from the tallest tree. Don't fire until you see the whites of their eyes![37]

—*American General Israel Putnam [at the Battle of Bunker Hill]*

The battle, sir, is not to the strong alone; it is to the vigilant, the active, the brave.[38]

—*Patrick Henry*

These are the times that try men's souls. The summer soldier and the sunshine patriot will, in this crisis, shrink from the service of his country; but he that stands it now, deserves the love and thanks of man and woman.[39]

—*Thomas Paine*

We have therefore to resolve to conquer or die: Our own country's honor, all call upon us for vigorous and manly exertion, and if we now shamefully fail, we shall become infamous to the whole world. Let us therefore rely upon the goodness of the Cause, and the aid of the Supreme Being, in whose hands victory is, to animate and encourage us to great and noble actions.[40]

—*George Washington*

I only regret that I have but one life to give for my country.[41]

—*Nathan Hale*

The hour is fast approaching, on which the honor and success of this army, and the safety of our bleeding country depend. Remember officers and soldiers, that you are freemen, fighting for the blessings of liberty—that slavery will be your portion, and that of your posterity, if you do not acquit yourselves like men.[42]

       —*George Washington*

George Washington
(February 22, 1732–December 14, 1799)

George Washington, popularly known as the "Father of His Country," served as the first president of the United States from 1789 to 1797. He was the commander in chief of the Continental Army during the Revolutionary War and presided over the writing of the Constitution. As a man of innumerable qualities, including tact, patience, compassion, and self-restraint, he was sought out by many for his counsel. He was by far the most popular and respected American politician of his time, and his leadership style and actions set many precedents for the Office of the President that have been continued to the present day. Although Washington was a respected executive, his service as military commander was probably his most significant contribution to his country. It is doubtful that any other military leader of his generation had the necessary forbearance, respect, and military acumen to defeat the British.

When we assumed the soldier, we did not lay aside the citizen.[43]

—*George Washington*

Yonder are the Hessians. They were bought for seven pounds and ten pence a man. Are you worth more? Prove it! Tonight the American flag floats from yonder hill or Molly Stark sleeps a widow![44]

—*American General John Stark [at the Battle of Bennington in 1777]*

These people show a spirit and conduct against us they never showed against the French…They are now spirited up by a rage and enthusiasm as great as ever people were possessed of, and you must proceed in earnest or give the business up.[45]

—*British General Sir Thomas Gage [to Britain's Secretary of War]*

O Lord of Hosts, lead forth thy servants of the American Army to battle and give them victory; or, if this be not according to Thy sovereign will, then, we pray Thee, stand neutral and let flesh and blood decide the issue![46]

> —*Israel Evans [chaplain of an American Brigade, immediately before battle]*

The passions of a revolution are apt to hurry even good men into excesses.[47]

> —*Alexander Hamilton*

We fight, get beat, and fight again.[48]

> —*American General Nathanael Greene*

It is a common observation here that our cause is the cause of all mankind, and that we are fighting for their liberty in defending our own.[49]

—*Benjamin Franklin*

Three millions of people, armed in the holy cause of liberty, and in such a country as that which we possess, are invincible by any force which our enemy can send against us. Beside, sir, we shall not fight our battles alone. There is a just God who presides over the destinies of nations, and who will raise up friends to fight our battles for us.[50]

—*Patrick Henry*

The rebels are not the despicable rabble too many have supposed them to be.[51]

—*British General Thomas Gage [to his superiors in London]*

We fight not to enslave, but to set a country free, and to make room upon the earth for honest men to live in.[52]

—*Thomas Paine*

Our cause is just, our union is perfect. Our internal resources are great, and, if necessary, foreign assistance is undoubtedly attainable… The arms we have been compelled by our enemies to assume, we will, in defiance of every hazard, with unabating firmness and perseverence, employ for the preservation of our liberties; being with one mind resolved to die freemen rather than live slaves.[53]

—*John Dickinson*

I know that the conquest of English
America is an impossibility. You cannot,
I venture to say it, you cannot conquer
America…If I were an American, as I am an
Englishman, while a foreign troop was landed
in my country, I would never lay down my
arms—never—never—never![54]

—*Sir William Pitt [speaking to Parliament]*

3

Liberty!

THE AGE OF Enlightenment is often credited with the rise of liberalism and republican values in America. Philosophers such as Britain's John Locke and France's Voltaire had promoted the concepts of liberty, equality, freedom of religion, and republicanism. American leaders embraced these ideas and developed a deepening distrust of kings and aristocracies. They became convinced that a virtuous and properly educated people could effectively rule themselves through a democratically elected republican government. The Founders believed that God had destined America to be a separate country, a beacon of liberty, and a model of better government for future generations. It was on these ideals that Thomas Jefferson based the Declaration of Independence—which was signed by the Second Continental Congress on July 4, 1776—over a year after the war began.

★★★

We hold these truths to be self-evident, that all men are created equal; that they are endowed by their Creator with inherent and unalienable rights; that among these are life, liberty, and the pursuit of happiness.[55]

—Declaration of Independence

It is the will of heaven that the two countries should be sundered forever. It may be the will of heaven that America shall suffer calamities still more wasting and distresses yet more dreadful. If this is to be the case, it will have this good effect, at least: it will inspire us with many virtues which we have not, and correct many efforts, follies, and vices, which threaten to disturb, dishonor and destroy us…The furnace of affliction produces refinements in states, as well as individuals.[56]

—John Adams

There! I guess King George will be able to read that![57]

> —*John Hancock [after signing his name in large script on the Declaration of Independence]*

☆☆☆

We must all hang together, or assuredly we shall all hang separately.[58]

> —*Benjamin Franklin [after signing the Declaration of Independence]*

☆☆☆

The distinctions between Virginians, Pennsylvanians, New Yorkers, and New Englanders are no more. I am not a Virginian, but an American![59]

> —*Patrick Henry*

For the support of this declaration, with a firm reliance on the protection of divine providence, we mutually pledge to each other our lives, our fortunes, and our sacred honor.[60]
—*Thomas Jefferson*

☆☆☆

Statesmen, my dear Sir, may plan and speculate for liberty, but it is religion and morality alone, which can establish the Principles upon which Freedom can securely stand.[61]
—*John Adams*

☆☆☆

He that would make his own liberty secure, must guard even his enemy from oppression; for if he violates this duty, he establishes a precedent that will reach to himself.[62]
—*Thomas Paine*

Liberty, when it begins to take root, is a plant of rapid growth.[63]

—*George Washington*

☆☆☆

Tyranny, like hell, is not easily conquered; yet we have this consolation with us, that the harder the conflict, the more glorious the triumph.[64]

—*Thomas Paine*

☆☆☆

The name of American, which belongs to you, in your national capacity, must always exalt the just pride of patriotism.[65]

—*George Washington*

Thomas Paine
(January 29, 1737–June 8, 1809)

*T*homas Paine was born in England and lived there until late 1774. In his thirties he became an excise officer, political activist, and writer who sought better pay and working conditions for the poor. Disillusioned with life in Britain and scornful of British government, he immigrated to the American colonies and soon began demonstrating his writing skills as editor of *The Pennsylvania Magazine*. In early 1776, he published the book *Common Sense*, which contributed to the spread of republican ideals, bolstered enthusiasm for independence from Britain, and encouraged recruitment for the Continental Army. *Common Sense* is still considered, proportionate to population, the most popular book ever published in America, and its significance cannot be overstated. For his inspirational writings, Thomas Paine is sometimes referred to as the "Father of the Revolution."

I have sworn upon the altar of God, eternal hostility against every form of tyranny over the mind of man.[66]

—*Thomas Jefferson*

Suspicion is a virtue as long its object is the preservation of the public good…Guard with jealous attention the public liberty. Suspect everyone who approaches that jewel.[67]

—*Patrick Henry*

We claim nothing but the liberty and privileges of Englishmen…we cannot be deprived of them, without our consent, but by violence and injustice; we have received them from our ancestors, and, with God's leave, will transmit them, unimpaired, to our posterity.[68]

—*George Mason*

Natural liberty is a gift of the beneficent Creator, to the whole human race; and… civil liberty is founded in that; and cannot be wrested from any people, without the most manifest violation of justice.[69]

—*Alexander Hamilton*

If our country, when pressed with wrongs at the point of the bayonet, had been governed by its heads instead of its hearts, where should we have been now? Hanging on a gallows as high as Haman's.[70]

—*Thomas Jefferson*

I believe there are more instances of the abridgment of the freedom of the people by gradual and silent encroachments of those in power, than by violent and sudden usurpations.[71]

—*James Madison*

Our cause is noble; it is the cause of mankind.[72]
    —*George Washington*

✩✩✩

No man in his senses can hesitate in choosing
to be free, rather than a slave.[73]
    —*Alexander Hamilton*

✩✩✩

No country upon earth ever had it more in
its power to attain these blessings than United
America. Wondrously strange, then, and much
to be regretted indeed would it be, were we to
neglect the means and to depart from the road
which Providence has pointed us to so plainly; I
cannot believe it will ever come to pass.[74]
    —*George Washington*

I would rather be exposed to the inconveniences attending too much liberty than those attending too small a degree of it.[75]

> —*Thomas Jefferson*

✩✩✩

One of the most essential branches of English liberty is the freedom of one's house. A man's house is his castle.[76]

> —*James Otis*

✩✩✩

Liberty can no more exist without virtue and independence than the body can live and move without a soul.[77]

> —*John Adams*

The sun never shined on a cause of greater worth. 'Tis not the affair of a city, a country, a province, or a kingdom, but of a continent—of at least one eighth part of the habitable globe. 'Tis not the concern of a day, a year, or an age; posterity are virtually involved in the contest, and will be more or less affected, even to the end of time, by the proceedings now. Now is the seed time of continental union, faith and honor.[78]

—*Thomas Paine*

☆☆☆

I wish to see all unjust and unnecessary discriminations everywhere abolished, and that the time may come when all our inhabitants of every color and discrimination shall be free and equal partakers of our political liberties.[79]

—*John Jay*

The welfare of America is intimately bound up with the happiness of humanity. She is going to become a cherished and safe refuge of virtue, of good character, of tolerance, of equality, and of a peaceful liberty.[80]

—*French General Marquis de Lafayette*

This was the object of the Declaration of Independence. Not to find out new principles, or new arguments, never before thought of, not merely to say things which had never been said before; but to place before mankind the common sense of the subject, in terms so plain and firm as to command their assent, and to justify ourselves in the independent stand we are compelled to take.[81]

—*Thomas Jefferson*

4

A More Perfect Union

THE DECLARATION OF Independence had presented a statement of ideology, but it had not established a system of government. To rectify this, in 1776, Congress began drafting the Articles of Confederation, intended to provide some degree of government during the war. But the Articles proved inadequate, and after the war, it became the task of the Founding Fathers to form a government that lived up to the ideologies expressed in the Declaration. The Founders knew that pure democracies had been attempted in the past, such as in ancient Greece, but had failed. Consequently, they turned to the republican form of democracy. They hotly debated the structure of administration and finally drafted a constitution that provided for three branches of federal government: legislative, judicial, and executive.

★★★

We the People of the United States, in order to form a more perfect union, establish justice, insure domestic tranquility, provide for the common defense, promote the general welfare, and secure the blessings of liberty to ourselves and our posterity, do ordain and establish this Constitution for the United States of America.[82]

—*Preamble to the United States Constitution*

☆☆☆

If men were angels, no government would be necessary. If angels were to govern men, neither external nor internal controls on government would be necessary. In framing a government which is to be administered by men over men, the great difficulty lies in this: you must first enable the government to control the governed; and in the next place oblige it to control itself.[83]

—*James Madison*

The care of human life and happiness, and not their destruction, is the first and only legitimate object of good government.[84]

—*Thomas Jefferson*

United we stand, divided we fall. Let us not split into factions which must destroy that union upon which our existence hangs.[85]

—*Patrick Henry*

The government we mean to erect is intended to last for ages.[86]

—*James Madison*

We are all Republicans, we are all Federalists. If there be any among us who would wish to dissolve this Union or to change its republican form, let them stand undisturbed as monuments to the safety with which error of opinion may be tolerated where reason is left free to combat it.[87]

—*Thomas Jefferson*

The advice nearest to my heart and deepest in my convictions is, that the Union of the States be cherished and perpetuated.[88]

—*James Madison*

The republican is the only form of government which is not eternally at open or secret war with the rights of mankind.[89]

—*Thomas Jefferson*

We are now forming a republican government. Real liberty is neither found in despotism
or the extremes of democracy, but in moderate
governments—if we incline too much to democracy, we shall soon shoot into a monarchy.[90]
       —Alexander Hamilton

It is much easier to pull down a government, in
such a conjuncture of affairs as we have seen, than
to build up, at such a season as the present.[91]
       —John Adams

*James Madison
(March 16, 1751–June 28, 1836)*

*J*ames Madison was the fourth president of the
United States from 1809 to 1817, secretary of state
under Thomas Jefferson, an influential member of
the U.S. House of Representatives, and an invaluable member of the Continental Congress. He was
instrumental in the drafting of the United States

Constitution and, as one of the three authors of *The Federalist Papers*, was a significant force in its adoption. He wrote the draft of the first twelve amendments to the Constitution, ten of which were ratified by the states. For these accomplishments, he is frequently referred to as both the "Father of the Constitution" and "Father of the Bill of Rights." Although he was initially a Federalist, he later broke ranks with Alexander Hamilton and joined with Thomas Jefferson to become a founder of the Democratic-Republican party.

In this situation of this Assembly, groping as it were in the dark to find political truth, and scarce able to distinguish it when presented to us, how has it happened, sir, that we have not hitherto once thought of humbly applying to the Father of Lights to illuminate our understanding?[92]

> —*Benjamin Franklin [at the Constitutional Convention]*

The great leading objects of the federal government, in which revenue is concerned, are to maintain domestic peace, and provide for the common defense.[93]

—*Alexander Hamilton*

Our Constitution was made only for a moral and religious people. It is wholly inadequate to the government of any other.[94]

—*John Adams*

☆☆☆

Although a republican government is slow to move, yet when once in motion, its momentum becomes irresistible.[95]

—*Thomas Jefferson*

The essence of Government is power; and power, lodged as it must be in human hands, will ever be liable to abuse.[96]

        —*James Madison*

I consider the government of the United States as interdicted by the Constitution from intermeddling with religious institutions, their doctrines, discipline, or exercises.[97]

        —*Thomas Jefferson*

There is not a man living who wishes more sincerely than I do, to see a plan adopted for the abolition of it [slavery].[98]

        —*George Washington*

The natural progress of things is for liberty to yield, and government to gain ground.[99]
—*Thomas Jefferson*

A national debt, if it is not excessive, will be to us a national blessing.[100]
—*Alexander Hamilton*

Every master of slaves is born a petty tyrant. They bring the judgment of Heaven on a country. As nations cannot be rewarded or punished in the next world, they must be in this. By an inevitable chain of causes and effects, Providence punishes national sins by national calamities.[101]
—*George Mason*

All, too, will bear in mind this sacred principle, that though the will of the majority is in all cases to prevail, that will to be rightful must be reasonable; that the minority possess their equal rights, which equal law must protect, and to violate would be oppression.[102]

—*Thomas Jefferson*

Wherever the real power in a government lies, there is the danger of oppression.[103]

—*James Madison*

[We are] the first people whom heaven has favoured with an opportunity of deliberating upon and choosing forms of government under which they should live.[104]

—*John Jay*

5

Faith

BELIEF IN RELIGIOUS freedom was a driving force in the American Revolution. Since many of their ancestors had traveled to the new world to escape religious discrimination, Americans expected to be able to worship God freely. When the Church of England became increasingly insistent on loyalty to the King, fear of renewed religious persecution increased. Consequently, ministers of other American churches assured their congregations that rebellion to the King was justified. After the war, freedom of worship was guaranteed to people of all faiths in the Bill of Rights. Today, the Founders are frequently misidentified as deists, who consider God to be a disinterested observer in the affairs of mankind. The majority of them were actually theistic rationalists or Christians, both of whom read the Bible and believe God answers prayer.

★★★

I've lived, sir, a long time, and the longer I live,
the more convincing proofs I see of this truth—
that God governs in the affairs of men.[105]

    —Benjamin Franklin

I have often expressed my sentiments, that
every man, conducting himself as a good citizen, and being accountable to God alone for
his religious opinions, ought to be protected in
worshipping the Deity according to the dictates
of his own conscience.[106]

    —George Washington

I must submit all my hopes and fears to an overruling Providence, in which, unfashionable as the faith may be, I firmly believe.[107]
—*John Adams*

All men are equally entitled to…the free exercise of religion, according to the dictates of conscience.[108]
—*James Madison*

Work as if you were to live 100 years, pray as if you were to die tomorrow.[109]
—*Benjamin Franklin*

Suppose a nation in some distant region should take the Bible for their only law book, and every member should regulate his conduct by the precepts there exhibited! Every member would be obliged in conscience, to temperance, frugality, and industry; to justice, kindness, and charity towards his fellow men; and to piety, love, and reverence towards Almighty God... What a Eutopia, what a Paradise would this region be.[110]

—*John Adams*

Providence has given to our people the choice of their rulers, and it is the duty as well as the privilege and interest of our Christian nation to select and prefer Christians for their rulers.[111]

—*John Jay*

My views…are the result of a life of inquiry and reflection, and very different from the anti-Christian system imputed to me by those who know nothing of my opinions. To the corruptions of Christianity I am, indeed, opposed; but not to the genuine precepts of Jesus himself. I am a Christian in the only sense in which he wished any one to be; sincerely attached to his doctrines in preference to all others.[112]

—*Thomas Jefferson*

May the Father of all mercies scatter light, and not darkness, upon our paths, and make us in all our several vocations useful here, and in His own due time and way everlastingly happy.[113]

—*George Washington*

Whilst we assert for ourselves a freedom to embrace, to profess, and to observe the religion which we believe to be of divine origin, we cannot deny an equal freedom to those whose minds have not yet yielded to the evidence which has convinced us. If this freedom be abused, it is an offence against God, not against man: To God, therefore, not to man, must an account of it be rendered.[114]

—*James Madison*

John Adams
(October 30, 1735–July 4, 1826)

*J*ohn Adams was the first vice president of the United States from 1789 to 1797 and the second president of the United States from 1797 to 1801. He was a leading political theorist, lawyer, statesman, and diplomat. He played a prominent role in persuading Congress to declare independence from Britain and assisted Thomas Jefferson in drafting the Declaration of Independence. Adams, Benjamin Franklin, and John Jay negotiated the Treaty of Paris, which formally ended the American Revolutionary War on September 3, 1783. He was the only member of the Federalist Party to ever become president. A lifelong rival of Thomas Jefferson, Adams expressed regret on his deathbed that Jefferson had outlived him. But Jefferson had passed a few hours earlier, fifty years to the day since signing the Declaration of Independence.

I take this early opportunity of…assuring you that I now exist and appear in the land of the living by the miraculous care of Providence, that protected me beyond all human expectation; I had 4 bullets through my coat, and two horses shot under me, and yet escaped unhurt.[115]

—*George Washington*

It is the duty of all men in society, publicly, and at stated seasons, to worship the Supreme Being, the great Creator and Preserver of the universe. And no subject shall be hurt, molested, or restrained, in his person, liberty, or estate, for worshipping God in the manner most agreeable to the dictates of his own conscience; or for his religious profession or sentiments; provided he doth not disturb the public peace, or obstruct others in their religious worship.[116]

—John Adams

A watchful eye must be kept on ourselves lest while we are building ideal monuments of renown and bliss here we neglect to have our names enrolled in the Annals of Heaven.[117]

—James Madison

One great advantage of the Christian religion is that it brings the great principle of the law of nature and nations, love your neighbor as yourself, and do unto others as you would that others should do to you, to the knowledge, belief, and veneration of the whole people.[118]

—*John Adams*

☆☆☆

We perceive that a great breach has been made in the moral and physical systems by the introduction of moral and physical evil; how or why, we know not; so, however, it is, and it certainly seems proper that this breach should be closed and order restored. For this purpose only one adequate plan has ever appeared in the world, and that is the Christian dispensation. In this plan I have full faith.[119]

—*John Jay*

I have thought proper to recommend, and I hereby recommend accordingly, that Thursday, the twenty-fifth day of April next, be observed throughout the United States of America as a day of solemn humiliation, fasting, and prayer; that the citizens on that day abstain, as far as may be, from their secular occupation, and devote the time to the sacred duties of religion, in public and in private; that they call to mind our numerous offenses against the most high God, confess them before Him with the sincerest penitence, implore his pardoning mercy, and through the Great Mediator and Redeemer, for our past transgressions, and that through the grace of His Holy Spirit, we may be disposed and enabled to yield a more suitable obedience to his righteous requisitions in time to come; that He would interpose to arrest the progress of that impiety and licentiousness in principle and practice so offensive to Himself and so ruinous to mankind; that He would make us deeply sensible that "righteousness exalteth a

nation but sin is a reproach to any people."
(Proverbs 14:34)[120]

> —*John Adams*

I...beg leave to move—that henceforth prayers
imploring the assistance of Heaven, and its
blessings on our deliberations, be held in this
Assembly every morning before we proceed to
business, and that one or more of the clergy of
this city be requested to officiate in that service.[121]

> —*Benjamin Franklin [prayers have opened*
> *sessions of Congress ever since Franklin's request*
> *on June 28, 1787]*

I have sometimes thought there could be
no stronger testimony in favor of religion or
against temporal enjoyments…than for men
who occupy the most honorable and gainful
departments and are rising in reputation and
wealth, publicly to declare their unsatisfactori-
ness by becoming fervent advocates in the cause
of Christ, & I wish you [William Bradford]
may give in your evidence in this way. Such
instances have seldom occurred, therefore they
would be more striking and would be instead of
a "Cloud of Witnesses."[122]

—*James Madison*

☆☆☆

I consider it an indispensable duty to close this
last solemn act of my official life by commending
the interest of dearest country to the protection
of Almighty God, and those who have the superintendence of them, to His holy keeping.[123]

—*George Washington*

For my own part, when I am employed in serving others, I do not look upon myself as conferring favours, but as paying debts. In my travels, and since my settlement, I have received much kindness from men, to whom I shall never have any opportunity of making the least direct return. And numberless mercies from God, who is infinitely above being benefited by our services. Those kindnesses from men, I can therefore only return on their fellow men; and I can only shew my gratitude for these mercies from God, by a readiness to help his other children and my brethren. For I do not think that thanks and compliments, tho' repeated weekly, can discharge our real obligations to each other, and much less those to our Creator.[124]

—*Benjamin Franklin*

And may that Being who is supreme over all, the Patron of Order, the Foundation of Justice, and the Protector in all ages of the world of virtuous liberty, continue His blessings upon this nation.[125]

—*John Adams*

Let us with caution indulge the supposition that morality can be maintained without religion…reason and experience both forbid us to expect that national morality can prevail in exclusion of religious principle.[126]

—*George Washington*

6

The People

Before the Revolution began, political theorists had debated the advantages of allowing a more learned, aristocratic class to govern. Some believed this was the only way to prevent uneducated, landless persons from attaining too much political power and jeopardizing the survival of democratic government. But the Founders had confidence in the American people and crafted a constitution that was both democratic and republican in form. The House of Representatives was elected by a direct vote of the people; the more experienced Senate was elected by members of the state legislatures. Today, both the House and Senate are elected directly by the people, and the Republic has survived the test of time. The preamble of the Constitution appropriately begins with the words "We the People of the United States…"

★★★

Only a virtuous people are capable of freedom. As nations become corrupt and vicious, they have more need of masters.[127]
—*Benjamin Franklin*

Government is instituted for the common good; for the protection, safety, prosperity, and happiness of the people; and not for profit, honor, or private interest of any one man, family, or class of men.[128]
—*John Adams*

The liberty enjoyed by the people of these states of worshiping Almighty God agreeably to their conscience, is not only among the choicest of their blessings, but also of their rights.[129]
—*George Washington*

The fabric of American empire ought to rest on the solid basis of the consent of the people. The streams of national power ought to flow from that pure, original fountain of all legitimate authority.[130]

—*Alexander Hamilton*

Every government degenerates when trusted to the rulers of the people alone. The people themselves, therefore, are its only safe depositories.[131]

—*Thomas Jefferson*

The people alone have an incontestable, unalienable, and indefeasible right to institute government; and to reform, alter, or totally change the same, when their protection, safety, prosperity, and happiness require it.[132]

—*John Adams*

No people can be bound to acknowledge and adore the Invisible Hand which conducts the affairs of men more than those of the United States. Every step by which they have advanced to the character of an independent nation seems to have been distinguished by some token of providential agency.[133]

—*George Washington*

Congress shall make no law respecting an establishment of religion, or prohibiting the free exercise thereof; or abridging the freedom of speech, or of the press; or the right of the people peaceably to assemble, and to petition the Government for a redress of grievances.[134]

—*First Amendment, U.S. Constitution*

The only foundation of a free constitution is pure virtue, and if this cannot be inspired into our people in a greater measure than they have it now, they may change their rulers and the forms of government, but they will not obtain a lasting liberty. They will only exchange tyrants and tyrannies.[135]

—*John Adams*

Your love of liberty—your respect for the laws—your habits of industry—and your practice of the moral and religious obligations, are the strongest claims to national and individual happiness.[136]

—*George Washington*

Cherish, therefore, the spirit of our people, and keep alive their attention. Do not be too severe upon their errors, but reclaim them by enlightening them. If once they become inattentive to the public affairs, you and I, and Congress, and assemblies, judges, and governors, shall all become wolves.[137]

—Thomas Jefferson

Benjamin Franklin
(January 17, 1706–April 17, 1790)

*B*enjamin Franklin earned the title of "The First American" as a result of his role as the senior statesman of the First and Second Continental Congresses, as well as his relentless campaigning for colonial unity before the Rebellion. He represented several colonies in

London prior to the American Revolution and was the first United States Ambassador to France during the Revolutionary War. Franklin was a world-renowned author, printer, scientist, inventor, and political theorist. He is famous for his experiments verifying that lightning is actually electricity and for his many inventions, including the lightning rod and bifocal glasses. In addition to his roles as First Minister to France and First Minister to Sweden, he was the first postmaster general of the United States. Toward the end of his life, he freed his slaves and became a prominent abolitionist.

A well-regulated Militia, being necessary to the security of a free state, the right of the people to keep and bear arms, shall not be infringed.[138]

—*Second Amendment, U.S. Constitution*

It should be the highest ambition of every American to extend his views beyond himself, and to bear in mind that his conduct will not only affect himself, his country, and his immediate posterity; but that its influence may be co-extensive with the world, and stamp political happiness or misery on ages yet unborn.[139]

—*George Washington*

I consider the war of America against Britain as the country's war, the public's war, or the war of the people in their own behalf, for the security of their natural rights, and the protection of their own property.[140]

—*Thomas Paine*

Above all things I hope the education of the common people will be attended to; convinced that on their good sense we may rely with the most security for the preservation of a due degree of liberty.[141]

— *Thomas Jefferson*

In 200 years will people remember us as traitors or heroes? That is the question we must ask.[142]

— *Benjamin Franklin*

Children should be educated and instructed in the principles of freedom.[143]

— *John Adams*

The right of the people to be secure in their persons, houses, papers, and effects, against unreasonable searches and seizures, shall not be violated, and no warrants shall issue, but upon probable cause, supported by oath or affirmation, and particularly describing the place to be searched, and the persons or things to be seized.[144]

—*Fourth Amendment, U.S. Constitution*

In proportion as the structure of a government gives force to public opinion, it is essential that public opinion should be enlightened.[145]

—*George Washington*

The powers not delegated to the United States by the Constitution, nor prohibited by it to the States, are reserved to the States respectively, or to the people.[146]

—*Tenth Amendment, U.S. Constitution*

I know no safe depository of the ultimate powers of the society but the people themselves; and if we think them not enlightened enough to exercise their control with a wholesome discretion, the remedy is not to take it from them, but to inform their discretion by education. This is the true corrective of abuses of constitutional power.[147]

—*Thomas Jefferson*

I must study politics and war that my sons may
have liberty to study mathematics and philosophy. My sons ought to study mathematics and
philosophy...in order to give their children a
right to study painting, poetry, music, architecture, statuary, tapestry, and porcelain.[148]
    —*John Adams*

It is on great occasions only, and after time has
been given for cool and deliberate reflection, that
the real voice of the people can be known.[149]
    —*George Washington*

The ultimate arbiter is the people of the Union.[150]
    —*Thomas Jefferson*

7

Character

THE FOUNDING FATHERS were concerned with the moral principles of the American people more than any other attribute. They were confident their countrymen would always be brave and industrious, but they feared a future decline in their moral character. This fear probably arose from what was known about previous democratic governments. The democracies of the ancient world had fallen apart due largely to a decline in the virtue of their citizens, the people's loss of interest in their voice in governmental decisions, or a lust for power by their leaders. The Founding Fathers believed that if the American people would remain honest, be attentive to their responsibilities as citizens, eschew personal fame and power, and love God, then America would remain a strong force for freedom and hope in the world.

Good moral character is the first essential in a man, and that the habits contracted at your age are generally indelible, and your conduct here may stamp your character through life. It is therefore highly important that you should endeavor not only to be learned but virtuous.[151]

—*George Washington*

Conscience is the most sacred of all property.[152]

—*James Madison*

I pronounce it as certain that there was never yet a truly great man that was not at the same time truly virtuous.[153]

—*Benjamin Franklin*

I love the man that can smile in trouble, that can gather strength from distress, and grow brave by reflection. 'Tis the business of little minds to shrink; but he whose heart is firm, and whose conscience approves his conduct, will pursue his principles unto death.[154]

—*Thomas Paine*

It should be your care, therefore, and mine, to elevate the minds of our children and exalt their courage; to accelerate and animate their industry and activity; to excite in them an habitual contempt of meanness, abhorrence of injustice and inhumanity, and an ambition to excel in every capacity, faculty, and virtue. If we suffer their minds to grovel and creep in infancy, they will grovel all their lives.[155]

—*John Adams*

I now make it my earnest prayer, that God would have you, and the state over which you preside, in His holy protection, that he would incline the hearts of the citizens to cultivate a spirit of subordination and obedience to government, to entertain a brotherly affection and love for one another, for their fellow citizens of the United States at large, and particularly for their brethren who have served in the field, and finally, that he would most graciously be pleased to dispose us all, to do justice, to love mercy, and to demean ourselves with that charity, humility, and pacific temper of mind, which were the characteristics of the Divine Author of our blessed religion, and without an humble imitation of whose example in these things, we can never hope to be a happy nation.[156]

—*George Washington*

Of all the dispositions and habits which lead
to political prosperity, religion and morality are
indispensable supports.[157]

—*George Washington*

It behooves you, therefore, to think and act for
yourself and your people. The great principles
of right and wrong are legible to every reader; to
pursue them requires not the aid of many coun-
selors. The whole art of government consists in
the art of being honest. Only aim to do your duty,
and mankind will give you credit where you fail.[158]

—*Thomas Jefferson*

Let them revere nothing but religion, morality,
and liberty.[159]

—*John Adams [in reference to his children]*

When you speak of God, or His attributes,
let it be seriously and with reverence. Honor and
obey your natural parents although they be poor.[160]
—*George Washington*

Alexander Hamilton
(January 11, 1755–July 12, 1804)

*A*lexander Hamilton was a soldier, economist, political philosopher, and constitutional lawyer. As the first United States Secretary of the Treasury under President George Washington, he had significant impact on founding American economic policy. He was the primary proponent of the establishment of a national bank, a system of tariffs, improved trade relations with Britain, and the funding of state debts. As founder of America's first political party, the Federalist Party, and one of the three authors of *The Federalist Papers*, Hamilton contributed significantly to the adoption of the United States Constitution. Hamilton was a close confidant of George Washington and succeeded him as Senior Officer of the Continental Army. Hamilton was killed in a duel with Vice President Aaron Burr in 1804, which was a result of a long-standing political rivalry and personal animosity.

Determine never to be idle. No person will have occasion to complain of the want of time, who never loses any. It is wonderful how much may be done, if we are always doing.[161]

—*Thomas Jefferson*

The foundations of national morality must
be laid in private families. In vain are schools,
academies, and universities instituted, if loose
principles and licentious habits are impressed
upon children in their earliest years.[162]
—*John Adams*

There is a certain enthusiasm in liberty that
makes human nature rise above itself, in acts of
bravery and heroism.[163]
—*Alexander Hamilton*

In reality there is perhaps no one of our natural
passions so hard to subdue as pride. Disguise it,
struggle with it, beat it down, stifle it, mortify it
as much as one pleases, it is still alive, and will
now and then peek out and show itself.[164]
—*Benjamin Franklin*

Adore God. Reverence and cherish your parents. Love your neighbor as yourself, and your country more than yourself. Be just. Be true. Murmur not at the ways of Providence. So shall the life into which you have entered be the portal to one of eternal and ineffable bliss.[165]

—*Thomas Jefferson*

Labor to keep alive in your breast that little spark of celestial fire called conscience.[166]

—*George Washington*

What we obtain too cheap, we esteem too lightly: it is dearness only that gives every thing its value.[167]

—*Thomas Paine*

It is of great importance to set a resolution, not
to be shaken, never to tell an untruth. There
is no vice so mean, so pitiful, so contemptible;
and he who permits himself to tell a lie once,
finds it much easier to do it a second and a
third time, till at length it becomes habitual;
he tells lies without attending to it, and truths
without the world's believing him. This false-
hood of the tongue leads to that of the heart,
and in time depraves all its good disposition.[168]
　　　　　　　　　—*Thomas Jefferson*

Judges, therefore, should be always men of
learning and experience in the laws, of exem-
plary morals, great patience, calmness, cool-
ness, and attention. Their minds should not be
distracted with jarring interests; they should not
be dependent upon any man, or body of men.[169]
　　　　　　　　　—*John Adams*

Everything is useful which contributes to fix in the mind principles and practices of virtue.[170]
—*Thomas Jefferson*

Having been poor is no shame, but being ashamed of it, is.[171]
—*Benjamin Franklin*

A nation which can prefer disgrace to danger is prepared for a master, and deserves one.[172]
—*Alexander Hamilton*

For avoiding the extremes of despotism or anarchy…the only ground of hope must be on the morals of the people. I believe that religion is the only solid base of morals and that morals are the only possible support of free governments.[173]

—*Gouverneur Morris*

☆☆☆

Give up money, give up fame, give up science, give the earth itself and all it contains rather than do an immoral act. And never suppose that in any possible situation, or under any circumstances, it is best for you to do a dishonorable thing, however slightly so it may appear to you…From the practice of the purest virtue, you may be assured you will derive the most sublime comforts in every moment of life, and in the moment of death.[174]

—*Thomas Jefferson*

8

Wisdom for the Ages

*I*T IS TRULY remarkable how far-sighted the Founding Fathers were. They understood the weaknesses of human nature and were well-informed on the advantages of democratically elected government. They knew that although they had done their best to establish a Constitution that would enable the Republic to survive future trials, it still had inherent weaknesses that could be exploited by power-hungry leaders. They foresaw that the machinery of government could become too large, that the military could become too weak, that the national debt could spiral out of control, that taxes could become too onerous, that laws could become too cumbersome, and that our efforts to help the poor and educate the young could become misdirected. They offered advice and sage warnings to all who would listen.

★★★

To be prepared for war is one of the most effectual means of preserving peace.[175]
—*George Washington*

☆☆☆

We must not let our rulers load us with perpetual debt.[176]
—*Thomas Jefferson*

☆☆☆

The form of government which communicates ease, comfort, security, or, in one word, happiness, to the greatest numbers of persons, and in the greatest degree, is the best.[177]
—*John Adams*

It will be of little avail to the people, that the laws are made by men of their own choice, if the laws be so voluminous that they cannot be read, or so incoherent that they cannot be understood; if they be repealed or revised before they are promulgated, or undergo such incessant changes that no man, who knows what the law is today, can guess what it will be tomorrow.[178]

—*Alexander Hamilton*

I think we have more machinery of government than is necessary, too many parasites living on the labor of the industrious.[179]

—*Thomas Jefferson*

I am for doing good to the poor, but I differ in opinion of the means. I think the best way of doing good to the poor, is not making them easy in poverty, but leading or driving them out of it. In my youth I traveled much, and I observed in different countries, that the more public provisions were made for the poor, the less they provided for themselves, and of course became poorer. And, on the contrary, the less was done for them, the more they did for themselves, and became richer.[180]

—*Benjamin Franklin*

Facts are stubborn things; and whatever may be our wishes, our inclination, or the dictates of our passions, they cannot alter the state of facts and evidence.[181]

—*John Adams*

Taxes should be proportioned to what may be annually spared by the individual.[182]
>   —*Thomas Jefferson*

The best and only safe road to honor, glory, and true dignity is justice.[183]
>   —*George Washington*

The spirit of resistance to government is so valuable on certain occasions, that I wish it to be always kept alive. It will often be exercised when wrong, but better so than not to be exercised at all. I like a little rebellion now and then. It is like a storm in the atmosphere.[184]
>   —*Thomas Jefferson*

Thomas Jefferson
(April 13, 1743–July 4, 1826)

Thomas Jefferson, known as the principal author of the Declaration of Independence, was the third president of the United States from 1801 to 1809, the first United States Secretary of State, and a diplomat to France who helped negotiate the Treaty of Paris, ending the American Revolutionary War. One of burgeoning America's leading political theorists, he spoke five languages and pursued interests in science, invention, farming, architecture, religion, and philosophy. He and James Madison established the Democratic-Republican Party in 1791, and today Jefferson is recognized as one of America's leading intellectuals of the Revolution. He had a lifelong rivalry with John Adams, and both of them seemed determined to outlive the other. Both he and Adams died on July 4, 1826—exactly fifty years after signing the Declaration of Independence. Adams outlived Jefferson by a few hours.

Honesty will be found on every experiment, to be the best and only true policy; let us then as a nation be just.[185]

—*George Washington*

In this world nothing can be said to be certain,
except death and taxes.[186]

—*Benjamin Franklin*

Associate yourself with men of good quality if
you esteem your own reputation; for 'tis better
to be alone than in bad company.[187]

—*George Washington*

The pleasures of this world are rather from
God's goodness than our own merit.[188]

—*Benjamin Franklin*

Charity is no part of the legislative duty of the
government.[189]

—*James Madison*

Were we directed from Washington [city] when to sow, and when to reap, we should soon want bread.[190]

—*Thomas Jefferson*

I hope, some day or another, we shall become a storehouse and granary for the world.[191]

—*George Washington*

Laws are made for men of ordinary understanding and should, therefore, be construed by the ordinary rules of common sense.[192]

—*Thomas Jefferson*

National defense is one of the cardinal duties
of a statesman.[193]
>   —*John Adams*

Human felicity is produced not so much by
great pieces of good fortune that seldom happen,
as by little advantages that occur every day.[194]
>   —*Benjamin Franklin*

It is better to offer no excuse than a bad one.[195]
>   —*George Washington*

Religion is the only solid basis of good morals;
therefore education should teach the precepts of
religion and the duties of man toward God.[196]
>   —*Gouverneur Morris*

It is infinitely better to have a few good men than many indifferent ones.[197]

—*George Washington*

☆☆☆

Let us tenderly and kindly cherish therefore, the means of knowledge. Let us dare to read, think, speak, and write.[198]

—*John Adams*

☆☆☆

Every difference of opinion is not a difference of principle. We have called by different names brethren of the same principle.[199]

—*Thomas Jefferson*

It is yet to be decided whether the Revolution must ultimately be considered as a blessing or a curse: a blessing or a curse, not to the present age alone, for with our fate will the destiny of unborn millions be involved.[200]

—*George Washington*

The duty of an upright administration is to pursue its course steadily, to know nothing of these family dissentions, and to cherish the good principles of both parties.[201]

—*Thomas Jefferson*

The Declaration of Independence…[is the] declaratory charter of our rights, and the rights of man.[202]

—*Thomas Jefferson*

I always consider the settlement of America with reverence and wonder, as the opening of a grand scene and design in Providence for the illumination of the ignorant, and the emancipation of the slavish part of mankind all over the earth.[203]

—*John Adams*

☆☆☆

Perseverance and spirit have done wonders in all ages.[204]

—*George Washington*

☆☆☆

The cause of America is in a great measure the cause of all mankind.[205]

—*Thomas Paine*

The Declaration of Independence

In Congress, July 4, 1776

THE UNANIMOUS DECLARATION of the thirteen united States of America,

When in the Course of human events, it becomes necessary for one people to dissolve the political bands which have connected them with another, and to assume among the powers of the earth, the separate and equal station to which the Laws of Nature and of Nature's God entitle them, a decent respect to the opinions of mankind requires that they should declare the causes which impel them to the separation.

We hold these truths to be self-evident, that all men are created equal, that they are endowed by their Creator with certain unalienable Rights, that among these are Life, Liberty and the pursuit of Happiness.—That to secure these rights, Governments are instituted among Men, deriving their just powers from the consent of the governed,—That whenever any Form of Government becomes destructive of these ends, it is the Right of the People to alter or to abolish it, and to institute new Government, laying its foundation on such principles and organizing its powers in such form, as to them shall seem most likely to effect their Safety and Happiness. Prudence, indeed, will dictate that Governments long established should not be changed for light and transient causes; and accordingly all experience hath shewn, that mankind are more disposed to suffer, while evils are sufferable, than to right themselves by abolishing the forms to which they are accustomed. But when a long train of abuses and usurpations, pursuing invariably the same Object evinces a design to reduce them under absolute Despotism, it is their right, it is their duty, to throw off such Government, and to provide new Guards for their future security.—Such has been the patient sufferance of these Colonies; and such is now the necessity which constrains them to alter their former Systems of Government. The history of the present King of Great Britain is a history of repeated injuries and usurpations, all having in direct object the establishment of an absolute Tyranny over these States. *[Note: the Founders' grievances against the King are not delineated here. For the entire Declaration of Independence, visit www.archives.gov]*

We, therefore, the Representatives of the united States of America, in General Congress, Assembled, appealing to the Supreme Judge of the world for the rectitude of our intentions, do, in the Name, and by Authority of the good People of these Colonies, solemnly publish and declare, That these United Colonies are, and of Right ought to be Free and Independent States; that they are Absolved from all Allegiance to the British Crown, and that all political connection between them and the State of Great Britain, is and ought to be totally dissolved; and that as Free and Independent States, they have full Power to levy War, conclude Peace, contract Alliances, establish Commerce, and to do all other Acts and Things which Independent States may of right do. And for the support of this Declaration, with a firm reliance on the protection of divine Providence, we mutually pledge to each other our Lives, our Fortunes and our sacred Honor.[206]

The fifty-six signatures on the Declaration:

Button Gwinnett	Thomas Nelson, Jr.
Lyman Hall	Francis Lightfoot Lee
George Walton	Carter Braxton
William Hooper	Robert Morris
Joseph Hewes	Benjamin Rush
John Penn	Benjamin Franklin
Edward Rutledge	John Morton
Thomas Heyward, Jr.	George Clymer
Thomas Lynch, Jr.	James Smith
Arthur Middleton	George Taylor
John Hancock	James Wilson
Samuel Chase	George Ross
William Paca	Caesar Rodney
Thomas Stone	George Read
Charles Carroll of Carrollton	Thomas McKean
George Wythe	William Floyd
Richard Henry Lee	Philip Livingston
Thomas Jefferson	Francis Lewis
Benjamin Harrison	Lewis Morris

Richard Stockton

John Witherspoon

Francis Hopkinson

John Hart

Abraham Clark

Josiah Bartlett

William Whipple

Samuel Adams

John Adams

Robert Treat Paine

Elbridge Gerry

Stephen Hopkins

William Ellery

Roger Sherman

Samuel Huntington

William Williams

Oliver Wolcott

Matthew Thornton

Samuel Adams's Speech to the Constitutional Convention in 1776

WE ARE NOW on this continent, to the astonishment of the world, three millions of souls united in one cause. We have large armies, well-disciplined and appointed, with commanders inferior to none in military skill, and superior in activity and zeal. We are furnished with arsenals and stores beyond our most sanguine expectations, and foreign nations are waiting to crown our success by their alliances. There are instances of, I would say, an almost astonishing Providence in our favor; our success has staggered our enemies, and almost given faith to infidels; so we may truly say it is not our own arm which has saved us.

The hand of Heaven appears to have led us on to be, perhaps, humble instruments and means in the great providential dispensation, which is completing. We have fled from the political Sodom; let us not look back, lest we perish and become a monument of infamy and derision to the world. For can we ever expect more unanimity and a better preparation for defense; more infatuation of counsel among our enemies, and more valor and zeal among ourselves? The same force and resistance, which are sufficient to procure us our liberties will secure us a glorious independence and support us in the dignity of free, imperial states. We cannot suppose that our opposition has made a corrupt and dissipated nation more friendly to America, or created in them a greater respect for the rights of mankind. We can therefore expect a restoration and establishment of our privileges, and a compensation for the injuries we have received, from their want of power, from their fears, and not from their virtues. The unanimity and valor, which will effect an honorable peace, can render a future contest for our liberties unnecessary. He who has strength to chain down the wolf is a madman if he let him loose without drawing his teeth and paring his nails.

We have no other alternative than independence, or the most ignominious and galling servitude. The legions of our enemies thicken on our plains; desolation and death mark their bloody career; whilst the mangled corpses of our countrymen seem to cry out to us as a voice from Heaven.

Our union is now complete; our constitution composed, established, and approved. You are now the guardians of your own liberties. We may justly address you, as the decemviri did the Romans, and say: "Nothing that we propose can pass into a law without your consent. Be yourselves, O Americans, the authors of those laws on which your happiness depends."

You have now in the field armies sufficient to repel the whole force of your enemies and their base and mercenary auxiliaries. The hearts of your soldiers beat high with the spirit of freedom; they are animated with the justice of their cause, and while they grasp their swords can look up to Heaven for assistance. Your adversaries are composed of wretches who laugh at the

rights of humanity, who turn religion into derision, and would, for higher wages, direct their
swords against their leaders or their country.
Go on, then, in your generous enterprise, with
gratitude to Heaven for past, success, and confidence of it in the future. For my own part, I ask
no greater blessing than to share with you the
common danger and common glory. If I have
a wish dearer to my soul than that my ashes
may be mingled with those of a Warren and a
Montgomery, it is that these American States
may never cease to be free and independent.[207]

General Washington's Speech of Resignation from the Army in 1783

December 23, 1783

THE GREAT EVENTS on which my resignation depended having at length taken place; I have now the honor of offering my sincere Congratulations to Congress and of presenting myself before them to surrender into their hands the trust committed to me, and to claim the indulgence of retiring from the Service of my Country.

Happy in the confirmation of our Independence and Sovereignty, and pleased with the opportunity afforded the United States of becoming a respectable Nation, I resign with satisfaction the Appointment I accepted with diffidence. A diffidence in my abilities to accomplish so arduous a task, which however was superseded by a confidence in the rectitude of our Cause, the support of the Supreme Power of the Union, and the patronage of Heaven.

The Successful termination of the War has verified the most sanguine expectations, and my gratitude for the interposition of Providence, and the assistance I have received from my Countrymen, increases with every review of the momentous Contest.

While I repeat my obligations to the Army in general, I should do injustice to my own feelings not to acknowledge in this place the peculiar Services and distinguished merits of the Gentlemen who have been attached to my person during the War. It was impossible the choice of confidential Officers to compose my family should have been more fortunate. Permit me Sir, to recommend in particular those, who have continued in Service to the present moment, as worthy of the favorable notice and patronage of Congress.

I consider it an indispensable duty to close this last solemn act of my Official life, by commending the Interests of our dearest Country to the protection of Almighty God, and those who have the superintendence of them, to his holy keeping.

Having now finished the work assigned me, I retire from the great theatre of Action; and bidding an Affectionate farewell to this August body under whose orders I have so long acted, I here offer my Commission, and take my leave of all the employments of public life.[208]

President Washington's Thanksgiving Proclamation of 1789

City of New York, October 3, 1789

Whereas it is the duty of all Nations to acknowledge the providence of Almighty God, to obey his will, to be grateful for his benefits, and humbly to implore his protection and favor, and Whereas both Houses of Congress have by their joint Committee requested me "to recommend to the People of the United States a day of public thanks-giving and prayer to be observed by acknowledging with grateful hearts the many signal favors of Almighty God, especially by affording them an opportunity peaceably to establish a form of government for their safety and happiness.

Now therefore I do recommend and assign Thursday the 26th. day of November next to be devoted by the People of these States to the service of that great and glorious Being, who is the beneficent Author of all the good that was, that is, or that will be. That we may then all unite in rendering unto him our sincere and humble thanks, for his kind care and protection of the People of this country previous to their becoming a Nation, for the signal and manifold mercies, and the favorable interpositions of his providence, which we experienced in the course and conclusion of the late war, for the great degree of tranquillity, union, and plenty, which we have since enjoyed, for the peaceable and rational manner in which we have been enabled to establish constitutions of government for our safety and happiness, and particularly the national One now lately instituted, for the civil and religious liberty with which we are blessed, and the means we have of acquiring and diffusing useful knowledge and in general for all the great and various favors which he hath been pleased to confer upon us.

And also that we may then unite in most humbly offering our prayers and supplications to the great Lord and Ruler of Nations and beseech him to pardon our national and other transgressions, to enable us all, whether in public or private stations, to perform our several and relative duties properly and punctually, to render our national government a blessing to all the People, by constantly being a government of wise, just and constitutional laws, discreetly and faithfully executed and obeyed, to protect and guide all Sovereigns and Nations (especially such as have shown kindness unto us) and to bless them with good government, peace, and concord. To promote the knowledge and practice of true religion and virtue, and the encrease of science among them and Us, and generally to grant unto all Mankind such a degree of temporal prosperity as he alone knows to be best.[209]

The Bill of Rights

THE PREAMBLE to the Bill of Rights
Congress of the United States begun and held at the City of New-York, on Wednesday the fourth of March, one thousand seven hundred and eighty nine.

THE Conventions of a number of the States, having at the time of their adopting the Constitution, expressed a desire, in order to prevent misconstruction or abuse of its powers, that further declaratory and restrictive clauses should be added: And as extending the ground of public confidence in the Government, will best ensure the beneficent ends of its institution.

RESOLVED by the Senate and House of Representatives of the United States of America, in Congress assembled, two thirds of both Houses concurring, that the following Articles be proposed to the Legislatures of the several States, as amendments to the Constitution of the United States, all, or any of which Articles, when ratified by three fourths of the said

Legislatures, to be valid to all intents and purposes, as part of the said Constitution; viz.

ARTICLES in addition to, and Amendment of the Constitution of the United States of America, proposed by Congress, and ratified by the Legislatures of the several States, pursuant to the fifth Article of the original Constitution.

Amendment I

Congress shall make no law respecting an establishment of religion, or prohibiting the free exercise thereof; or abridging the freedom of speech, or of the press; or the right of the people peaceably to assemble, and to petition the Government for a redress of grievances.

Amendment II

A well-regulated Militia, being necessary to the security of a free State, the right of the people to keep and bear Arms, shall not be infringed.

Amendment III

No Soldier shall, in time of peace be quartered in any house, without the consent of the Owner, nor in time of war, but in a manner to be prescribed by law.

Amendment IV

The right of the people to be secure in their persons, houses, papers, and effects, against unreasonable searches and seizures, shall not be violated, and no Warrants shall issue, but upon probable cause, supported by Oath or affirmation, and particularly describing the place to be searched, and the persons or things to be seized.

Amendment V

No person shall be held to answer for a capital, or otherwise infamous crime, unless on a presentment or indictment of a Grand Jury, except in cases arising in the land or naval forces, or in the Militia, when in actual service in time of War or public danger; nor shall any person be subject for the same offence to be twice put in jeopardy of life or limb; nor shall be compelled in any criminal case to be a witness against himself, nor be deprived of life, liberty, or property, without due process of law; nor shall private property be taken for public use, without just compensation.

Amendment VI

In all criminal prosecutions, the accused shall enjoy the right to a speedy and public trial, by an impartial jury of the State and district wherein the crime shall have been committed, which district shall have been previously ascertained by law, and to be informed of the nature and cause of the accusation; to be confronted with the witnesses against him; to have compulsory process for obtaining witnesses in his favor, and to have the Assistance of Counsel for his defence.

Amendment VII

In Suits at common law, where the value in controversy shall exceed twenty dollars, the right of trial by jury shall be preserved, and no fact tried by a jury, shall be otherwise re-examined in any Court of the United States, than according to the rules of the common law.

Amendment VIII

Excessive bail shall not be required, nor excessive fines imposed, nor cruel and unusual punishments inflicted.

Amendment IX

The enumeration in the Constitution, of certain rights, shall not be construed to deny or disparage others retained by the people.

Amendment X

The powers not delegated to the United States by the Constitution, nor prohibited by it to the States, are reserved to the States respectively, or to the people.[210]

Endnotes

1. John Adams letter to H. Niles, February 13, 1818.
2. Speech at Second Virginia Convention, St. John's Church in Richmond, VA, on March 23, 1775.
3. Thomas Jefferson letter to John Randolph, November 29, 1775.
4. Bobrick, Benson. (2011). *Angel in the Whirlwind: The Triumph of the American Revolution.* New York: Simon & Schuster, p. 75.
5. Franklin, Benjamin. (1818). *Memoirs of the Life and Writings of Benjamin Franklin, Written by Himself.* Philadelphia: William Duane, p. 352.
6. Paine, Thomas. (1776). *Common Sense*, initially published anonymously.
7. Forbes, Estcher. (1942). *Paul Revere and the World He Lived In.* Cambridge, MA, p. 374.
8. Speech on the Stamp Act, Virginia House of Burgesses, May 29, 1765.
9. Bobrick, p. 77.
10. Bancroft, George (1838). *Bancroft's History of the United States of America, vol. II.* Boston: Little and Brown, p. 229.
11. Bowers, Claude G. (1945). *The Young Jefferson, 1743–1789.* New York: Houghton Mifflin, p. 41.
12. Wood, Gordon S. (2002). *The American Revolution: A History.* New York: Modern Library, p. 55.
13. General Orders, July 2, 1776.

14. John Adams letter to William Cushing, June 9, 1776.
15. Bobrick, p. 66. Jefferson borrowed this from Benjamin Franklin.
16. Adams, Samuel. (1772). *The Rights of the Colonists*, pamphlet.
17. Paine, *Common Sense*.
18. Patrick Henry. Speech at Second Virginia Convention, St. John's Church in Richmond, VA, on March 23, 1775.
19. Paine, Thomas. (1776). *The American Crisis*, No. 1, pamphlet.
20. Jefferson, Thomas. (1774). *A Summary of the View of the Rights of British America*. Williamsburg: Clementina Rind, p. 20.
21. Adams, John. (1765). "A Dissertation on the Canon and Feudal Law," first published in the *Boston Gazette*.
22. Speech at Second Virginia Convention, St. John's Church in Richmond, VA, on March 23, 1775.
23. Hamilton, Alexander. (1775). *The Farmer Refuted*, pamphlet.
24. Paine, *Common Sense*.
25. Adams, *The Rights of the Colonists*.
26. Jefferson, Thomas. (1785). *Notes on the State of Virginia*, Query 18. Initially published anonymously, in Paris.
27. John Adams letter to Abigail Adams, July 17, 1775.
28. Paine, *Common Sense*.
29. McCullough, David. (2005). *1776*. New York: Simon & Schuster, p. 6.
30. Hibbert, Christopher. (2000). *George III: Personal History*. New York: Basic Books, p. 145.

31. Speech at Second Virginia Convention, St. John's Church in Richmond, VA, on March 23, 1775.

32. Coburn, Frank W. (1922). *The Battle of April 19, 1775: In Lexington, Concord, Lincoln, Arlington, Cambridge, Somerville, and Charlestown, Massachusetts*. Lexington, MA: Lexington Historical Society, p. 63.

33. Brooks, Victor (1999). *The Boston Campaign*. Conshohocken, PA: Combined Publishing.

34. Sherburne, John Henry. (1825). *The Life and Character of John Paul Jones, a Captain in the United States Navy*. New York: Adriance, Sherman, and Company. The source of this quote is Richard Dale, Jones's first lieutenant in the battle between the British ship *Serapis* and the American ship *Bonhomme Richard*. Other sources disagree on the exact words, but not the spirit, of Captain Jones's response to the question the British Captain had shouted, asking if Jones was going to surrender.

35. Burnett, Edmund Cody, ed. (1921–36). *Letters of Members of the Continental Congress*, in 8 volumes. Vol 1. Washington, D.C., p. 138.

36. Bobrick, p. 165.

37. Swett, Samuel. (1815). *History of Bunker Hill Battle, With a Plan*. Boston: Annin and Smith, p. 17. This quote is usually attributed to General Israel Putnam and may also have been said by other officers at the Battle of Bunker Hill (also referred to as Breed's Hill). It had been a common admonition to troops awaiting battle and was not original to Putnam.

38. Speech at Second Virginia Convention, St. John's Church in Richmond, VA, on March 23, 1775.

39. Paine, *The American Crisis*, No. 1.

40. General Orders, July 2, 1776.

41. Attributed last words (September 22, 1776), according to the account by American officer William Hull based on reports by British Captain John Montresor, who was present at the hanging and had spoken to Hull under a flag of truce the following day.

42. General Orders, August 23, 1776.

43. Hudleston, F. J. (1927). *Gentleman Johnny Burgoyne*. Garden City, NY, p. 204.

44. Ibid.

45. Gage, Thomas. (1931–1933). *The Correspondence of General Thomas Gage*, in two volumes. Vol. 2. New Haven, CT, p. 686–7.

46. Bobrick, p. 180.

47. Syrett, Harold, ed. (1961). *The Papers of Alexander Hamilton*, vol. I. Columbia University Press, p. 129.

48. Nathanael Greene letter to George Washington, May 1, 1781.

49. Benjamin Franklin letter to Samuel Cooper, May 1, 1777.

50. Speech at Second Virginia Convention, St. John's Church in Richmond, VA, on March 23, 1775.

51. Davidson, Marshall B. (1975). *The Horizon History of the World in 1776*. New York, p. 321.

52. Paine, *The American Crisis*, No. 4.

53. Dickinson, John. (1775). *The Declaration of the Causes and Necessity on Taking up Arms*. Printed by the Second Continental Congress.

54. Montross, Lynn. (1950). *The Reluctant Rebels*. New York: Harper and Brothers, p. 231.

55. The Declaration of Independence.

56. John Adams letter to Abigail Adams, July 3, 1776.

57. Unger, H. G. (2000). *John Hancock: Merchant King and American Patriot*, New York: John Wiley, p. 241.

58. Sparks, Jared. (1840). *The Works of Benjamin Franklin*. Quote attributed to Benjamin Franklin at the signing of the Declaration of Independence, July 4, 1776.

59. Patrick Henry. Speech in the First Continental Congress, Philadelphia, October 14, 1774.

60. The Declaration of Independence.

61. Adams, Charles Francis, ed. (1865). *The Works of John Adams, Second President of the United States, with a Life of the Author, 1850–1856*, ten volumes. Vol. IX. Boston: Little, Brown, and Company, p. 401.

62. Paine, Thomas. (1791). *Dissertation on First Principles of Government*.

63. George Washington letter to James Madison, March 2, 1788.

64. Paine, *The American Crisis*, No. 1.

65. George Washington. *Farewell Address*, September 19, 1796.

66. Thomas Jefferson letter to Benjamin Rush, September 23, 1800.

67. Patrick Henry. Speech on the Federal Constitution, Virginia Ratifying Convention, 1768.

68. Rowland, Kate Mason. (1892). *Life of George Mason*, New York: G. P. Putnam's Sons, p. 387.

69. Syrett, Harold, ed. (1961). *The Papers of Alexander Hamilton*, vol. I. Columbia University Press, p. 104.

70. Thomas Jefferson letter to Maria Cosway, 1786.

71. James Madison. Speech at the Virginia Convention to ratify the Federal Constitution, June 6, 1788.

72. George Washington letter to James Warren, March 31, 1779.

73. Hamilton, Alexander. (1774). *A Full Vindication of the Measures of the Congress*, pamphlet.

74. George Washington letter to Benjamin Lincoln, June 29, 1788.

75. Thomas Jefferson letter to Archibald Stewart, December 23, 1791.

76. Otis, James. (1761). "Against Writs of Assistance," reprinted in *The Annals of America*, Encyclopedia Britannica, Inc. (1976), vol. 2, 1755–83 Resistance and Revolution selection #15, p. 75.

77. Bailyn, Bernard, ed. (1965). *Pamphlets of the American Revolution*, vol. 1, 1750–65. Cambridge, MA, p. 55.

78. Paine, *Common Sense*.

79. John Jay letter to Dr. Benjamin Rush, March 24, 1785. Quoted in Linda M. Freeman. (2005). *Selected Letters of John Jay and Sarah Livingston Jay: Correspondence by or to the First Chief Justice of the United States and His Wife*, p. 170.

80. Woodward, W. E. (1938). *Lafayette*. New York, p. 33.

81. Thomas Jefferson letter to Henry Lee, May 8, 1825.

82. From the National Archives, www.archives.gov.

83. *The Federalist Papers* No. 51. *The Federalist Papers* were originally published as articles in either the *Independent Journal* or the *New York Packet*, between 1787 and 1788. In 1788, they were published by J. and A. McLean in two bound volumes, known as *The Federalist*.

84. Thomas Jefferson letter to the Republican Citizens of Washington County, Maryland, March 31, 1809.

85. Henry, William Wirt. (1891). *Patrick Henry: Life, Correspondences and Speeches, Vol. 2.* New York: Charles Scribner's Sons, p. 609–10.

86. Yates, Robert. From June 26, 1787 statement, as quoted in *Notes of the Secret Debates of the Federal Convention of 1787.*

87. Jefferson's first inaugural address.

88. Mattern, David B. (1997). *James Madison's Advice to My Country,* University of Virginia Press, p. 104.

89. Thomas Jefferson letter to William Hunter, March 11, 1790.

90. Debates of the Federal Convention, June 26, 1787.

91. John Adams letter to James Warren, 1787.

92. Benjamin Franklin. Speech proposing prayers in the convention, June 28, 1787.

93. Alexander Hamilton. Remarks in the New York Ratifying Convention, June 1788.

94. Adams, Charles F. (1854) *The Works of John Adams, Second President of the United States,* Boston: Little, Brown, and Company, p. 229.

95. Thomas Jefferson letter to Francis C. Gray, 1815.

96. Speech on the Virginia Constitutional Convention, December 2, 1829. Hunt, Galliard. (1910). *The Writings of James Madison: 1819–1836.* New York: G. P. Putnam's Sons, p. 361.

97. Thomas Jefferson letter to Samuel Miller, January 23, 1808.

98. George Washington letter to Robert Morris, April 12, 1786.

99. Thomas Jefferson letter to Edward Carrington, May 27, 1788.

100. Alexander Hamilton letter to Robert Morris, April 30, 1781.

101. Madison, James. (1908). *The Journal of the Debates in the Convention which Framed the Constitution of the United States, May–September, 1787*, vol. 2. New York: G. P. Putnam's Sons.

102. Jefferson's first inaugural address.

103. James Madison letter to Thomas Jefferson, October 17, 1788.

104. Wood, p. 65.

105. Benjamin Franklin. Speech proposing prayers in the convention, June 28, 1787.

106. George Washington letter to the General Committee of the United Baptist Churches in Virginia, May 1789.

107. John Adams letter to Abigail Adams, July 3, 1776.

108. Brookhiser, Richard (2011). *James Madison*. New York: Basic Books, p. 24.

109. Franklin, Benjamin. (1758). *Poor Richard Improved*, pamphlet.

110. John Adams diary entry, February 22, 1756.

111. John Jay letter to John Murray, October 12, 1816.

112. Thomas Jefferson letter to Dr. Benjamin Rush, April 24, 1803.

113. George Washington letter to the Hebrew Congregation of Newport, RI, August 17, 1790.

114. 1785 session of the General Assembly of the State of Virginia: Religious Freedom, A Memorial and Remonstrance.

115. George Washington letter to his brother, John A. Washington, on July 18, 1755.

116. Adams, John. (1776). *Thoughts on Government*, pamphlet.

117. James Madison letter to William Bradford, November 9, 1772.

118. John Adams diary entry, August 14, 1796.

119. John Jay letter to Lindley Murray, August 22, 1774.

120. Adams, John. Proclamation of National Fast Day, March 6, 1799.

121. Benjamin Franklin. Speech to the Continental Congress, June 28, 1787.

122. James Madison letter to William Bradford, September 1773, quoted in *The Lustre of Our Country: The American Experience of Religious Freedom* (2000) by John Thomas Noonan, p. 66.

123. George Washington's address to Congress at Annapolis, December 23, 1783. Washington's official resignation of his military commission.

124. Benjamin Franklin letter to Joseph Huey, June 6, 1753.

125. John Adams's inaugural address, March 4, 1797.

126. Washington's farewell address.

127. Benjamin Franklin letter dated April 17, 1787.

128. Adams, *Thoughts on Government*.

129. George Washington. Speech to the annual meeting of Quakers, September 1789.

130. *The Federalist Papers* No. 22.

131. Jefferson, Thomas. (1781). *Notes on the State of Virginia*, Query 14.

132. Adams, *Thoughts on Government*.

133. Washington's first inaugural address, April 30, 1789.

134. The Bill of Rights, Article I.

135. John Adams letter to Zabdiel Adams, June 21, 1776.

136. George Washington letter to the Residents of Boston, October 27, 1789.

137. Thomas Jefferson letter to Edward Carrington, January 16, 1787.

138. The Bill of Rights, Article 2.

139. George Washington letter to the Legislature of Pennsylvania, September 5, 1789.

140. Paine, *The American Crisis*.

141. Thomas Jefferson letter to James Madison, December 20, 1787.

142. Benjamin Franklin letter to Thomas Jefferson, March 16, 1775.

143. Adams, John. (1787). *A Defense of the Constitutions of Government of the United States of America*, originally published in London in 3 volumes.

144. The Bill of Rights, Article 4.

145. Washington's farewell address.

146. The Bill of Rights, Article 10.

147. Thomas Jefferson letter to William Charles Jarvis, September 28, 1820.

148. John Adams letter to Abigail Adams, 1780.

149. George Washington letter to Edward Carrington, May 1, 1796.

150. Thomas Jefferson letter to William Johnson, 1823.

151. George Washington letter to George Steptoe Washington, December 5, 1790.

152. Madison, James. (1792). "Property essay."

153. Benjamin Franklin. *The Busy-body, No. 3*, February 18, 1728.

154. Paine, *The American Crisis*, No. 1.

155. Adams, *A Dissertation on the Canon and Feudal Law*.

156. George Washington. *Circular Letter of Farewell to the Army*, June 8, 1783.

157. Washington's farewell address.

158. Jefferson, Thomas. (1774). *A Summary of the View of the Rights of British America*. Williamsburg: Clementina Rind, p. 20.

159. John Adams letter to Abigail Adams, April 15, 1776.

160. Washington, George. (Reprint 1971). *Rules of Civility & Decent Behaviour in Company and Conversation: A Book of Etiquette*. Williamsburg, VA: Beaver Press.

161. Thomas Jefferson letter to Martha Jefferson, May 5, 1787.

162. John Adams diary entry, June 2, 1778.

163. Hamilton, *The Farmer Refuted*.

164. Franklin, Benjamin. (1771). *The Autobiography of Benjamin Franklin*. Originally published in Paris.

165. Thomas Jefferson letter to Thomas Jefferson Smith, February 21, 1825.

166. Washington, *Rules of Civility*.

167. Paine, *The American Crisis*, No. 1.

168. Thomas Jefferson letter to Peter Carr, August 19, 1785.

169. Adams, *Thoughts on Government*.

170. Bowers, Claude G. (1945). *The Young Jefferson, 1743–1789*. New York: Houghton Mifflin, p. 24.

171. Franklin, Benjamin. (1749). *Poor Richard's Almanac*, pamphlet.

172. Alexander Hamilton letter to the *Daily Advertiser*, February 21, 1797.

173. Gouverneur Morris letter to Lord George Gordon, June 28, 1792.

174. Thomas Jefferson letter to Peter Carr, August 19, 1785.

175. George Washington's first annual message to Congress, January 8, 1790.

176. Thomas Jefferson letter to Samuel Kercheval, July 12, 1816.

177. Adams, Charles Francis, ed. (1865). *The Works of John Adams, Second President of the United States, with a Life of the Author, 1850–1856*, ten volumes. Boston: Little, Brown, and Company.

178. *The Federalist Papers* No. 62.

179. Thomas Jefferson letter to William Ludlow, September 6, 1824.

180. Benjamin Franklin. *On the Price of Corn and Management of the Poor*, November 1766.

181. John Adams. Defense of the British soldiers on trial for the Boston Massacre, December 4, 1770.

182. Thomas Jefferson letter to James Madison, December 8, 1784. From Paul Leicester Ford, ed., *The Works of Thomas Jefferson* in twelve volumes, Vol. 4. Federal Edition. (1904–5). New York and London: G. P. Putnam's Sons.

183. George Washington letter to Marquis de Lafayette, September 30, 1779.

184. Thomas Jefferson letter to Abigail Adams, February 22, 1787.

185. George Washington. *Circular letter to the States*, June 14, 1783.

186. Benjamin Franklin letter to Jean-Baptiste Leroy, November 13, 1789. Quoted in *Bartlett's Familiar Quotations*, p. 321.

187. Washington's Rules of Civility.

188. Franklin, Benjamin. (1748). *Proposal for Pennsylvania's First Day of Fasting.*

189. James Madison. Speech to the House of Representatives during the debate "On the Memorial of the Relief Committee of Baltimore, for the Relief of St. Domingo Refugees," January 10, 1794.

190. Jefferson, Thomas. (1821). *Autobiography.*

191. George Washington letter to Marquis de Lafayette, June 19, 1788.

192. Thomas Jefferson letter to William Johnson, June 12, 1823.

193. John Adams letter to James Lloyd, January 1815.

194. Franklin, Benjamin. (1771). *Autobiography.*

195. George Washington letter to Harriet Washington, October 30, 1791.

196. Sparks, Jared. (1832). *The Life of Gouverneur Morris, vol. 3.* Boston: Gray and Bowen, p. 483, from his "Notes on the Form of a Constitution for France."

197. George Washington letter to James McHenry, August 10, 1798.

198. Adams, *A Dissertation on the Cannon and Feudal Law.*

199. Jefferson's first inaugural address.

200. George Washington. *Circular to the States,* 1783.

201. Thomas Jefferson letter to George Logan, 1805.

202. Thomas Jefferson letter to Samuel Adams Wells, May 12, 1821.

203. Adams, *A Dissertation on the Cannon and Feudal Law.*

204. George Washington letter to General Philip Schuyler, August 20, 1775.

205. Paine, *Common Sense.*

206. Excerpt of the Declaration of Independence. See
     www.archives.gov for the entire document.

207. Excerpt of a speech by Samuel Adams on August 1,
     1776, presented to the Continental Congress in the
     State House in Philadelphia.

208. Speech by General George Washington, made before
     the Congress of the Confederation in Annapolis,
     MD, on December 23, 1783, resigning his commis-
     sion as commander-in-chief of the Army.

209. Proclamation of Thanksgiving by President George
     Washington, observed on November 26, 1789.

210. From the National Archives, www.archives.
     gov. These are the first ten amendments to the
     Constitution in their original form. These amend-
     ments were ratified December 15, 1791, and formu-
     late what is today known as the "Bill of Rights."

Online Resources

When an endnote lists a private letter or public paper as the source for the quote, the reader can access this material at one of the following online resources:

George Washington:

The George Washington Papers at the Library of Congress:
http://memory.loc.gov/ammem/mgwquery.html

The Papers of George Washington: http://gwpapers.virginia.edu/

Thomas Jefferson:

The Thomas Jefferson Papers at the Library of Congress:
http://memory.loc.gov/ammem/collections/jefferson_papers/

University of Virginia Collection of Thomas Jefferson:
http://guides.lib.virginia.edu/TJ

John Adams:

Massachusetts Historical Society: www.masshist.org/publications/apde/search.php

The Adams Papers Digital Edition: http://rotunda.upress
.virginia.edu/founders/ADMS.html

BENJAMIN FRANKLIN:

The Papers of Benjamin Franklin: www.franklinpapers
.org/franklin/

ALEXANDER HAMILTON:

The Papers of Alexander Hamilton: http://rotunda.upress
.virginia.edu/founders/ARHN.html

JAMES MADISON:

The James Madison Papers at the Library of Congress:
http://memory.loc.gov/ammem/collections/madison
_papers/

The Papers of James Madison Digital Edition: http://
rotunda.upress.virginia.edu/founders/JSMN.html

PATRICK HENRY:

Executive Papers of Patrick Henry: http://ead.lib.virginia
.edu/vivaxtf/view?query=give+me+liberty&docId=lva%
2Fvi00438.xml&chunk.id=

THOMAS PAINE:

The Writings of Thomas Paine: http://oll.libertyfund.org
/index.php?option=com_staticxt&staticfile=show.php
?title=1743&Itemid=27

FEDERALIST PAPERS:

The Federalist Papers online: www.foundingfathers.info
/federalistpapers/

DECLARATION OF INDEPENDENCE, CONSTITUTION,
AND BILL OF RIGHTS:

The National Archives online: www.archives.gov/

About the Editor

Gordon Leidner has been a lifelong student of American history. He is a board member of the Abraham Lincoln Institute and maintains the popular history website www.greatamerican history.net. Through the Great American History website, he has provided numerous articles and free educational material about the American Civil War and the American Revolution since 1996. Leidner lives near Annapolis, Maryland, with Jean, his wife of thirty-four years.

If you enjoyed this book, please consider *Abraham Lincoln: Quotes, Quips, and Speeches*, also by Gordon Leidner.